Everyday Clothes
through History

by
Fiona MacDonald

GARETH**STEVENS**
GS
PUBLISHING
A Member of the WRC Media Family of Companies

Please visit our Web site at: www.garethstevens.com
For a free color catalog describing Gareth Stevens Publishing's
list of high-quality books and multimedia programs, call
1-800-542-2595 (USA) or 1-800-387-3178 (Canada).
Gareth Stevens Publishing's fax: (414) 332-3567.

Library of Congress Cataloging-in-Publication Data

McDonald, Fiona, 1942-
     Everyday clothes through history / by Fiona McDonald.
         p. cm. — (Why do we wear?)
     Includes index.
     ISBN-10: 0-8368-6853-6 — ISBN-13: 978-0-8368-6853-1 (lib. bdg.)
     1. Clothing and dress—History—Juvenile literature. I. Title. II. Series.
GT518.M35   2007
391.009—dc22   2006017496

This North American edition first published in 2007 by
Gareth Stevens Publishing
A Member of the WRC Media Family of Companies
330 West Olive Street, Suite 100
Milwaukee, Wisconsin 53212 USA

This edition copyright © 2007 by Gareth Stevens, Inc. Original edition copyright © 2006
by ticktock Entertainment Ltd. First published in Great Britain by ticktock Media Ltd.,
Unit 2 Orchard Business Centre, North Farm Road, Tunbridge Wells, Kent TN2 3XF.

Managing editor: Valerie J. Weber
Gareth Stevens editor: Gini Holland
Gareth Stevens art direction: Tammy West
Gareth Stevens designer: Kami Strunsee

Picture Credits (t=top, b=bottom, l=left, r=right, c=center)
Bridgeman Art Library: 15t, 15b, 23b; CORBIS: 4-5 b, 14-15, 16 all, 17 all; 24 all, 25b, 26t; 27 all, 28t;
Library of Congress Collection: 23t, 25t; Rex Features: 22b, 26b; ticktock Entertainment: 5t, 5c, 6t, 12t, 12b,
13t, 13b, 20 all, 21 all, 22t, 28b, 29 all;Werner Forman Archive: 6b, 8t, 8-9, 9t, 9b, 10t, 10bl, 10br, 11t, 11b,
18t, 18-19, 19t, 19c; We Ought to Know: 14t.

Every effort has been made to trace the copyright holders, and we apologize in advance for any unintentional omission.
We would be pleased to insert the appropriate acknowledgements in any subsequent edition of this publication.

Printed in the United States of America

1 2 3 4 5 6 7 8 9 10 09 08 07 06

Cover: Actress Kate Winslet models an everyday dress popular in the 1800s.

Words that appear in the glossary are printed in
boldface type the first time they occur in the text.

Introduction

Many animals, such as cats, groom their fur. Pigs smother themselves in mud. Insects spin **cocoons**. Humans, however, are the only creatures to create coverings for their bodies that can be removed, reworn, and replaced.

Belonging

Clothes can show which tribe or nation we belong to. They may also reveal our gender and whether we are married or single. Clothes can make a political statement or proclaim our religion. They can give onlookers clues about the work we do, how much money we have, and the image we hope to create for ourselves.

The skirt worn by this Masai woman from East Africa shows that she is married and belongs to a wealthy family.

More than Useful

Clothes are useful. They shield our skin and protect us from scratches and bruises. They keep us warm and dry or cool and comfortable. They cheer us with bright colors and pamper us with soft textures. More than this, clothes serve as signs of our identity. They send out messages about us, describing our place in the world.

Members of the same age group often choose similar clothes.

Traditional or Modern?

Today, many different kinds of clothes are worn all round the world. Some, like an *abayah* or a *hijab,* are traditional. They are based on ancient designs belonging to one particular group of people. Others, such as jeans and T-shirts, have a much shorter history. They were created within the past hundred years and can only be made by modern machines.

This young woman is wearing a modern version of traditional Muslim hijab (modest dress).

Everyday Clothes

In the past, most ordinary people could only afford one set of clothes at a time. They wore them every day. Compared with elaborate fashions, worn only by rich people, everyday clothes were practical and long lasting. Their designs changed very slowly. Most were worn — and mended — year after year, until they finally fell to pieces.

These working-class boots were made in the late 1890s.

What happened to very old everyday clothes?

5

The First Everyday Clothes

N o one knows exactly when the first clothes were made. Many historians think clothing was invented some time between 50,000 B.C. and 100,000 B.C. This was the time when modern humans (*Homo sapiens*) left their warm homeland in Africa and migrated to live in colder parts of the world.

Furs and Hides

The first clothes were made from the furs or hides (skins) of large wild animals. Early peoples preserved the skins by rubbing them with fat or hanging them over a smoky fire. After about 30,000 B.C., clothes makers used stone knives to trim skins and, to sew them together, they used needles of bone or mammoth ivory

Furs and skins were sewn by pushing a needle through holes made by a sharp-pointed blade.

These Sioux war leggings date from the late eighteenth century.

Tunics and Trousers

The first sewn garments were sleeveless **tunics** worn by men or women. They were made from two animal skins, cut, shaped, and stitched together at the shoulders. Wearers went bare legged or wrapped their feet and legs with strips of animal skin. Trousers were invented later, between 20,000 B.C. and 10,000 B.C.

What were furs and skins sewn together with ?

The earliest woven garments were sheep's wool blankets. They looked similar to the traditional blankets worn by Masai men in Africa today.

Squeezing and Weaving

Early people also created clothes by working with natural fibers. They twisted tall plant stems into string and hammered tree bark to make fabric. They made **felt** by boiling and squeezing animal hair and spun thread by twirling plant fibers or sheep's wool. At first, string and thread were only used for nets, bags, and braids. Later, thread was woven into cloth on wooden frames called looms.

Silk and Cotton

Around 3,000 B.C., people living in India and China found ways of creating finer, more delicate fibers. Chinese workers unwound miles of natural silk thread from cocoons made by silk-moth grubs (silkworms) and wove the threads into shimmering gauze, which is a thin, transparent fabric. At the same time, Indus Valley farmers harvested fluffy cotton wool (the fiber around cotton seeds), spun it into thread, and then wove it into light, cool cloth.

Indian saris (long lengths of fabric carefully folded at the waist and draped around the body) were some of the earliest clothes to be made from cotton — and later silk.

Ancient Egypt and Its Neighbors

The climate of Egypt, in North Africa, is hot and very dry. Because of this, the Ancient Egyptians wore very few clothes. They were, however, some of the earliest men and women to wear clothing made from woven fabric, instead of from animal skins and furs.

This wall painting of Ramses III shows him wearing a loincloth.

Simple Shapes

Egyptian clothes were simple — just lengths of fabric folded into convenient shapes and then pinned or tied around the body. For working in their fields, Egyptian men wore brief **loincloths** (strips of fabric wrapped between the legs like a diaper) or short lengths of fabric wound around the waist, like kilts (wrapped skirts). Both styles were held in place by knotting two ends of the garment together or by belts made of leather or rope.

Unchanging Styles

Women's clothing was made of a larger piece of cloth wrapped right around the body from the breast to the ankle. Sometimes, two small pieces were used instead and stitched together at the sides. Both methods created a long, narrow, tube-shaped garment, which was kept from slipping down by two wide shoulder straps. It stayed in style for almost 2,000 years.

A straight, simple, narrow dress was everyday wear for most Egyptian women. Natural cream and white (for linen) and tan or gray (for wool) were the usual shades.

Sleeves and Pleats

After around 1530 B.C., invaders from West Asia
brought new clothing designs to Egypt. Men
and women began to wear extra lengths of fabric
draped loosely over their arms and shoulders.
These created wide, baggy sleeves and were held
in place, front and back, by tight waist belts or
metal pins. Men also began to wear double-layer
kilts with extra front and side panels. Pleated
clothes draped gracefully, trapped cool air close
to the body, and let the wearer move freely.

The Egyptian man on the
left wears a kilt with a
wide, pleated front panel.
The man on the right
wears a simpler, old-style
kilt, tied at the waist.

Furs and Fringes

At night, when desert temperatures fell quickly, Egyptian men and
women wrapped themselves in warm blankets woven from sheep's
wool. Their neighbors in colder, mountainous lands of West
Asia continued to wear thick, bulky cloaks of
sheepskin and fur. These Asians also wove
woolen cloth decorated with fringes and
tassels to look like shaggy animal skins.

What was the Egyptians' favorite fabric?

This Sumerian carved pillar
shows King Hammurabi
(*left*) wearing a heavy cloak
typical of the style of the
eighteenth century B.C.

Ancient Greece and Rome

Greek traders traveled throughout the Mediterranean region, picking up clothing fashions along the way. Greek clothes were made of Greek sheep's wool, Turkish linen, and even silk imported from China.

Greek farmers dressed in traditional himations.

Cloaks and Tunics

On the Greek mainland, the everyday dress for men was a knee-length **chiton** (tunic), made of woolen fabric that was sewn or pinned at the shoulders and the sides. In cold weather, a *chamlys* (short cloak) or **himation** (long cloak) was worn on top. Old men and men in authority often wore long tunics that reached to the ground.

Graceful and Comfortable

Greek women's clothes were made in a similar way to men's from long, unshaped lengths of cloth. The most common women's garment was the **peplos**, made by pinning a length of cloth at the shoulders, then binding it close to the body with a **girdle** (a band of braid or ribbon) tied around the waist and below the breasts. Outside the home, Greek women also wore a himation and used part of it to veil their heads and faces.

The woman (*left*) wears a long, flowing peplos. Like many Greek children, her son is naked, except for a chiton (short cloak) around his shoulders.
The city-state of Sparta was famous for the freedom given to its women (*right*) — and for the short, manlike clothes they wore.

The Romans' home in central Italy was close to Ancient Greek lands across the narrow Ionian Sea. Like Greek clothes, early Roman garments were just lengths of fabric folded to fit the body.

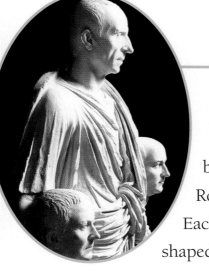

This ancient statue is called *Barberini Man Wearing a Toga*. The man carries busts of two ancestors.

Toga, Toga

The earliest Roman garment was the **toga**. Originally, it was the only piece of clothing Roman men and women wore, but by around 200 B.C., it had become a sign of Roman citizenship and was restricted to men only. Each toga was a huge, heavy woolen cloak, shaped like a half circle.

Ready for Work

A long, heavy toga made it difficult for the wearer to move quickly or do hard physical work. So, from around 200 B.C., most ordinary Roman men — and slaves — wore short tunics, similar to the Greek chiton. Underneath, they wore loincloths. On top, when it was cold, they wore blankets or short, hooded cloaks.

A Roman soldier's short tunic makes movement easy.

The Layered Look

Roman women's tunics were floor-length, draped, and tied with decorative girdles. Often, they wore two or more tunics at the same time. Eventually, the outer tunic became known as a *stola*. Over their tunics, women wore a long cloak, called a *palla*, and, sometimes, a veil.

How did Greeks make clothes fit each wearer?

Women's underwear included a lightweight loincloth and a supportive band of cloth around the breasts, called a *mammilare*.

Medieval Europe

At the start of the Middle Ages, people in southern Europe wore clothes similar to old Roman ones. Slowly, new ways of making clothes were invented. These new ways created dramatically different new styles.

Typical Tunics

In Europe, a T-shaped tunic remained the standard male garment. It was, however, cut and sewn in a neater, less bulky shape than in previous centuries. It now had long sleeves and was worn with a thick cloak for warmth. It was belted round the waist. In northern Europe, men also wore baggy trousers.

This eleventh-century illustration shows a wine seller dressed in a typical tunic of the time.

Surcoats and Wimples

Early medieval women wore long, loose, tunic-shaped dresses, sewn with side seams and with long wide sleeves. Underneath, they wore a long **chemise** (loosely fitting, tunic-shaped dress). On top, they often wore a sleeveless **surcoat** (overdress), cut and sewn in different local designs, plus a heavy woolen cloak in winter weather. Married women covered their hair with scarves, veils, or **wimples** (a wide band of cloth hiding the neck and reaching up to the chin).

This Viking woman, from about A.D. 1050, is wearing a long chemise topped by a two-piece overdress, or surcoat.

A.D. 500 – 1500

Fit and Flare

By about A.D. 1300, artisans in European cities had developed new tailoring skills. For the first time in Europe, men and women wore clothes with tight **bodices** (coverings for the top half of the torso) and separate, sewn-in sleeves. Men's tunics and women's dresses had flared skirts, with narrow waists and wide, sweeping hems.

A female servant in Italy, about A.D. 1350, wears a dress with a tightly fitted bodice, flared skirt, low neckline, and narrow, tailored sleeves.

Dull Colors

Everyday clothes worn by ordinary people began to be made in these new, fitted styles. Unlike bright, patterned clothes worn by the rich, however, they only appeared in plain colors. This was because ordinary people could not afford exotic imported fabrics, or expensive colored dyes. Their everyday clothes were made from rough, homespun wool or linen, in natural shades of cream, gray, or brown or colored with muted, earthy plant dyes.

A north European family, about A.D. 1480, wears stylishly shaped but dull-colored clothing.

Asia

Throughout most of Asia, ordinary people in the past worked outdoors as farmers, growing crops on the land or tending flocks of sheep and cattle. Their everyday clothes had to protect them from extreme weather conditions.

Travellers on the Arabian Peninsula wore long, flowing tunics.

Loose and Cool

In many parts of western Asia, men and women wore long, loose, flowing tunics with wide sleeves. On top, they each wore a robe that was called a *jubba* in Syria and given other names in other countries. The tunics were simply made from lengths of cloth stitched together without tailoring. Fabrics included cotton, linen, and wool.

"It's a Wrap!"

In India, ancient wrapped styles continued to prove useful for thousands of years. Indian women folded and draped extremely long lengths of cloth into graceful, colorful saris, which many still wear today. Indian men wore a **dhoti**, a rectangle of cloth that could be wrapped like a skirt or wound between the legs to create loose, baggy pants. Similar styles developed in Southeast Asia, where they were worn by men and women and are called **sarongs**.

Statues from a temple, carved about A.D. 1200, show worshippers wearing long, wrapped dhotis.

Kaftans and Pants

In northwest India and neighboring lands, everyday clothes developed from garments worn by the ancient Persians. The most important was the **kaftan**, a fitted, long-sleeved coat, opening down the front, usually worn over pants. Kaftans became popular from Turkey to Mongolia. Persian-style baggy pants also spread to northwest India (now Pakistan), where women wore them with long tunics. Today, this combination is known as *salwar kameez.*

This early eighteenth century print shows a Persian man from the Ottoman Empire.

For Chinese Workers

Traditionally, ordinary Chinese people wore long robes that wrapped in front or short jackets that fastened in front. They tied both styles with a sash around the waist and paired the jackets with long cotton or linen skirts or loose pants. When Manchu invaders from the north conquered China in 1644, they forced Chinese workers to wear clothes similar to Manchu styles. These included long, loose robes with wide sleeves and high collars.

These Chinese tea packers, painted about A.D. 1750, are wearing traditional Chinese jackets, wide pants, and sashes.

Africa

In most of Africa, the climate is warm all year round. Much of the land south of the Sahara is covered with dense rain forest or tall grasses and bushes. In traditional societies, men and women lead active lives. Tight, complex clothes would stop them from traveling far or working well. Children often go naked for the first few years of life.

Bark and Leather

The earliest African clothes were made of natural substances. For example, in southern and east-central Africa, leather from hunted animals or specially treated tree bark was made into aprons. These were worn in pairs, at the front and the back of the body, by men and unmarried girls. Married women wore a leather skirt and cloak.

Leather garments were often decorated with fringes, strips of animal fur, or beads.

Wrapped Cloth

The first woven cloth in Africa was made about 3000 B.C. Over the centuries, African weavers became very skillful at spinning thread from wool, goat hair, or plant fibers such as raffia; dying it in brilliant colors; and weaving it into cloth. They also obtained rough silk thread by unwrapping African moth cocoons. Most garments were not cut or sewn but just draped and tied around the body. Wrapped styles included simple blanket cloaks worn by East African cattle herders and pure white wrap-around robes worn in Ethiopia.

Fastened at the shoulder, this East African cloak leaves both hands free for work.

A Nigerian man wears a traditional wrapped cloth tunic.

Robes and Slings

In crop-growing and trading communities, especially in West Africa, wrapped clothes became more elaborate as individual wealth increased and people could afford more fabric. Successful men wore full wrap-around robes draped in impressive, dignified styles. New designs for men appeared, such as the tunic made from a length of folded cloth with an opening for the head. West African women wore long wrapped skirts or full-length wrap dresses. They also made slings by winding lengths of cloth around their backs so they could carry their babies and leave their hands free.

Modest and Practical

In North Africa, harsh desert conditions made nakedness uncomfortable. Long robes protected people from blowing sand and intense sunlight. After about A.D. 700, a new religion made covering the body important for most North African people. Islam teaches that men and women alike should be modestly dressed. Many North Africans converted to Islam. Muslim soldiers from Asia also brought new styles with them, especially pants. For many North African men, these became everyday wear under long, loose robes. North African women also wore long robes topped by cloaks and wide, gauzy scarves or veils.

North Africans make their robes from a long length of fabric, folded in two, which they leave partly open on either side of the body. The openings serve as sleeves and also provide some coolness.

Early Americas

Early humans first reached Alaska, in the far northwest of North America, some time before 35,000 B.C. Slowly, they spread south, reaching the tip of South America by about 9000 B.C. Different groups settled in separate areas and developed their own styles of clothing for everyday wear.

Soft, Warm Fleece

American clothes were made from materials that were available locally. These varied widely from place to place. Some were found only in America. In the high Andes Mountains region, Inca women wove **ponchos** (thick cloaks, like blankets with a hole for the head) from the soft, warm fleece of native llama and alpaca, dyed in vivid colors. Ponchos were worn by men over knee-length tunics woven from plant fibers. Incan women wore loose, straight-sided, ankle-length dresses.

The Incas mummified dead bodies. They wrapped them in woven blankets and ponchos.

Pelts and Furs

In the icy Arctic regions of North America, Inuit and Aleut peoples made clothes from the skins of animals they hunted for food: deer, caribou, polar bears, seals, and foxes. These animals all had thick, shaggy, waterproof coats that had evolved to help them survive in bitter weather. Arctic men and women all wore similar garments: a hooded tunic, called a **parka** or **anorak**, and pants and boots. In winter, they added extra tunics, called *kuletaks*.

This women's dress, made by the Native American Sioux people, is decorated with quills on the bodice.

Skins, Tails, and Paws

Other Native Americans also made clothes from animal skins. After cleaning, drying, and softening the skins, they sewed them together to make tunics for men or long dresses for women. At first, clothing makers left the animals' manes, tails, or paws in position as decoration. Later, they cut the skins to shape the clothes and added colorful trimmings such as brightly dyed porcupine quills.

This European portrait of an Inuit man from Alaska shows him dressed from head to toe in fur-lined clothes.

Settlers' clothes included tailored coats and knee breeches for men, and long, full-skirted dresses for women.

Which trade goods, brought by Europeans, replaced quills as decoration for clothes?

Settler Styles

When the first Europeans arrived to settle in North America, they brought clothing styles from their homelands with them. Their life in the "New World" was harsh, and many disapproved of finery for religious reasons. They wore tough, durable clothes, in dark colors, made from thick cloth and leather.

Europe 1500–1750

After about 1500, European clothing styles began to change more quickly. Clothes were very expensive, however, so many people chose new garments for their hard-wearing qualities, as well as for their appearance. An outfit was expected to last for at least ten years.

Rich and Poor

Rich people followed the latest fashions. In the sixteenth century, these featured tight corsets, stiffened skirts, **trunk hose** (baggy shorts, fastened tightly round the thigh), and padded **doublets** (jackets). Ordinary peoples' clothes copied the fashionable shapes but were looser and lighter. Men wore simple knee-length breeches, and women's skirts ended above the ankle.

Behind the Times

In the seventeenth century, ordinary peoples' clothes continued to follow the fashion of the rich. Men's jackets became longer, covering the hips, and so did their pants, which extended below the knee. Under their jackets, men wore a collarless shirt and, often, a sleeveless waistcoat, or vest. In some regions, such as Highland Scotland, kilts (male skirts) were still worn. Ordinary women continued to wear long dresses with

This fashionable silk dress was worn by a wealthy noblewoman in about 1740.

These girls are dressed in sixteenth-century style. Their dresses (worn over long-sleeved chemises) have low, square necks, narrow waists, and long, full skirts.

close-fitting bodices. Underneath, they wore chemises and petticoats. For extra warmth, men and women wore cloaks. Women also wore shawls and kerchiefs.

Political Styles

Everyday clothes carried a political message, especially in eighteenth-century France. Poor people, who often went hungry, were outraged to see the extravagant clothes worn by wealthy nobles. In return, rich politicians criticized the poor for being dressed in rags. French protesters, dressed in ordinary, everyday clothes, were nicknamed **sans-culottes**, which means "without culottes." They did not wear — and could not afford — the fashionable, **tailored** culottes, or knee breeches.

In seventeenth-century Britain, most royal courtiers wore clothes trimmed with ribbons, lace, and bows. Ordinary people wore plainer styles.

Homespun Clothes

Ordinary men and women could not afford fashionable materials, such as lace, muslin (fine cotton), silk, and velvet. They wore linen, hemp, and wool. Often, cloth was woven from thread spun from local sheep's fleece by ordinary women in their homes. They sold their homespun thread to traveling merchants, who resold it to weavers in towns.

This early printed picture shows protesters attacking nobles in knee breeches (*left*) and two poor people (*far right*) in ragged everyday clothes.

1500 – 1750

Western World 1750–1900

New inventions transformed everyday clothing after about 1750. Sewing machines meant that clothes could be stitched together faster than ever. Railways and cheap newspapers spread details of the latest fashions to ordinary people throughout Europe and the United States.

Cotton for All

Originally, cotton was a rare, precious cloth imported to Europe from India. By the mid-nineteenth century, new steamships carried vast quantities of raw cotton to European factories, where it was spun, woven, and sewn on machines to make cheap clothing for everyday wear. In the United States, cotton was grown on southern plantations worked by slaves, then sent to northern cities for processing.

Cotton absorbed sweat and was cool and comfortable, especially in hot working environments, such as iron foundries and factories.

Work Wear and Underwear

Cotton clothes soon became popular for among working families. Cotton was much easier to wash than old-style wool, and far quicker to dry. Machine-made cotton garments were cheap, too. Cotton was used to make tough clothes for male workers, such

This replica cotton dress, made of carefully sewn, costly fabric, would have been worn by a fashionable, wealthy woman in about 1810.

This nineteenth-century farmworker is wearing a long-sleeved chemise, fitted bodice, and full skirt.

as full-length pants and aprons, and also for men's shirts and underpants. For women, cotton cloth was sewn into blouses, camisoles (sleeveless tops worn next to the skin), aprons, petticoats, and underpants.

Country Traditions

Before sewing machines were invented, cotton clothes were sewn by hand, usually in women's homes. In the countryside, working people continued to make many of their own everyday clothes by hand, using traditional materials and following traditional styles. Increasingly, however, they traveled to towns to buy machine-made clothing.

This picture from a fashion magazine shows the latest styles for women's shawls (*left*) and dresses (*right*) in about 1900.

Fashion for All

By about 1900, cheap, machine-made garments — together with fashion magazines — brought the latest styles closer to ordinary people. Women especially became much more fashion-conscious. They wanted their everyday clothes to look up-to-date, yet still be practical to wear. They looked for fashion details, such as high, "choker" necklines, when they bought sensible new outfits. Many added fashionable trimmings, such as braid and lace, to existing everyday clothes.

When were sewing machines invented?

Western World 1900–1950

In the early twentieth century, new technology continued to increase the range of cheap, mass-produced everyday clothes for ordinary people. Clothing styles still followed high fashion, but styles were also influenced by social changes, economic crises, and two world wars.

Regional Variations

In poor regions such as southern Europe, women wore dresses with tight bodices and long skirts. Men wore long, straight pants with shirts and jackets or vests. Fishermen and sailors preferred hand-knitted woolen sweaters. In the western United States, farmhands and cowboys dressed in shirts and narrow pants made of tough blue denim — the first blue jeans, patented by Levi Strauss in the 1870s.

These women wear aprons and shawls over their dresses as they wash clothes at an Italian street fountain in 1907. The boy wears pants and a knitted sweater.

Wartime and "Flappers"

During World War I (1914–1918), millions of men were in uniform. Off duty, they wore clothes similar to late nineteenth-century peacetime styles, including three-piece suits for office work and woolen jackets with thick pants for farmers. Women's clothes changed dramatically as they took over fighting men's jobs, such as driving trains and working in factories. For ease of movement and for safety, they took off their stiff, wasp-waisted corsets and cut their skirts "short," about 8 inches (20 cm) off the ground. After the war, **flappers** wore loose, fun clothes they could dance in.

A stylishly dressed woman of the Flapper Era (1920s) models a loose-fitting, sleeveless dress and feather boa.

Work and Leisure

In the 1920s and 1930s, male laborers working in factories, at construction sites, and on farms, wore all-in-one heavy cotton overalls. Men employed in shops and offices dressed in neat suits and

These American workers pictured in the 1920s wear casual clothing.

1900 – 1950

ties. For leisure wear, most men chose similar styles — relaxed, baggy pants and a loose jacket or knitted sweater. Zippers, which were mass-produced beginning in the 1930s, replaced buttons and buckles for leisure wear.

Uniform Styles

Women's dresses in the 1930s became slightly longer and more fitted as a reaction to the 1920s boyish styles. In 1939, World War II began. Large numbers of women volunteered to join the armed forces, and, even off duty, their everyday clothes were based on sensible, masculine, uniform styles. Skirts were the shortest yet (knee length), with crisp pleats. Dresses had collars like uniforms, and jackets were short and square-shouldered, like those worn by men.

During World War II, legs were often bare, because silk and fine cotton, used for stockings, were in short supply. Women wore jackets that reminded them of the fighting men they missed.

Western World 1950–2000

In the second half of the twentieth century, all kinds of clothing, from everyday garments to high-fashion designs, changed more quickly than ever before. Ideas about wearing clothes changed as well. There were fewer rules about "correct" or "suitable" dressing.

Plain and Simple

In the 1950s, women wore heels for everyday wear.

Many countries in Europe were devastated by World War II. Clothing was scarce and hard to buy, and many governments rationed fibers and fabrics even after the war and added high taxes to luxury imports. They also encouraged citizens to not throw old, worn clothes away. Men's suits and women's dresses were plain and simple and used no unnecessary fabric. In spite of this new "**utility**" style, women still wore high heels for everyday wear and put on hats and gloves when going out.

"Made in the USA"

In the 1940s and 1950s, the United States became the world leader in popular entertainment. As a result, blue jeans, seen in cowboy movies, began to be sold beyond western states in the 1950s. American knitted cotton sportswear, such as polo shirts and T-shirts, replaced shirts made of **broadcloth** (woven fabric) for informal, everyday occasions. Comfortable but form-fitting knitted-cotton briefs were favorite underwear for both men and women. By the 1960s, new, artificial fibers, such as nylon (invented by U.S. chemists) were used for everyday clothes.

Marlon Brando sports a T-shirt in *A Streetcar Named Desire*.

The most famous 1960s garment was the mini-skirt, worn six inches above the knee, pioneered by alternative British designer, Mary Quant.

Anything Goes

The 1960s were a time of social experiment and political discontent. Young people rebelled against authority, including school dress codes, and chose their own everyday clothes. These combined the latest high-fashion designs with shapes, fabrics, and decorations from many ethnic traditions.

Which undergarment became popular because of mini-skirts?

For the first time, trends in everyday clothing were set by ordinary men and women, not by the rich. Although it caused protests, women also began to wear pants as ordinary, everyday clothes.

Sportswear Spin-Offs

Everyday wear based on comfortable sports clothes was first made by French designer Coco Chanel in the 1920s and 1930s. By the end of the twentieth century, mass-produced versions of sports-style clothes, such as jogging suits and sweatshirts, were the Western world's most popular everyday leisure wear. New elastic fibers, such as Lycra, invented in the U.S. in 1959, were added to knitted or woven fabrics during manufacture. They gave a much closer fit, fewer wrinkles, and extra flexibility.

Sports clothes were first worn by young people but were soon chosen by older men and women, as well.

1950 – 2000

Global Styles Today

Today, Western media and Western-based corporations dominate world communications and world trade. Their power has helped spread Western social attitudes and visual styles all around the globe. Because of this, in many societies everyday clothes are now much less formal than before.

Peer-Group Pressure

Following trends set in the 1960s, today's young people mostly like to wear similar styles. Wearing different clothes can lead to criticism or rejection by their **peers** (equals). In the same way, men and women choose tailored suits for everyday office wear, worldwide. Other global everyday clothes are chosen for practicality. For example, many workers still wear overalls, although they are often made of artificial fibers rather than cotton.

Young peoples' everyday clothes include jeans, shorts, T-shirts, sleeveless tops, and halter tops.

This Quechua woman is shown wearing traditional everyday clothing.

Maintaining Tradition

In some parts of the world, people still prefer to wear traditional clothes everyday. This is the case in many Muslim countries, where religious beliefs encourage all men and women to be modestly and traditionally dressed. Alternatively, some Muslims may choose Western clothes for home but cover them with a traditional robe when they go outdoors. In other regions, such as India, Africa, and South America,

In recent years, companies and social activists have worked together to end sweatshop conditions, such as those seen in this factory in Mumbai, India.

traditional styles are still sometimes preferred, especially for important occasions. People with strong ethnic traditions often feel proud of past everyday clothing styles, even though they might not wear them all the time.

What material was added to jeans in the 1990s?

Fair-Price Clothing

Today, international corporations build factories in developing countries where wages are low and building costs are less expensive than in Europe or the United States. This practice creates cheaper clothing, because many workers in developing countries are poorly paid and exploited. Clothing makers in developed countries often lose their jobs because they cannot compete with these poorly paid workers. Governments struggle with trade arrangements, trying to regulate imports and exports and achieve a fair exchange.

International Brands

International clothing brands have caused controversy. They are popular with consumers and widely admired. On the other hand, many regret the disappearance of traditional garments and unique styles as people increasingly prefer global brands.

By purchasing popular brands, consumers decide what today's global everyday clothes will be.

Costume historians and folklore experts now collect examples of old-style everyday clothes to study and preserve in museums.

Glossary

abayah long, loose robe worn in Arab countries

anorak hooded, fur-lined tunic, worn by the Inuit people of the Eastern Arctic region

artisans people who make jewelry, pottery, or other crafted items

bodices garments (or a part of a garment) covering the upper part of the body from the shoulders to the waist

broadcloth cloth woven on a loom

chamlys ancient Greek short cloak

chemise long tunic, made of fine woven fabric, worn as an undergarment from the Middle Ages until the nineteenth century

chiton ancient Greek short tunic

cocoons outer casing, usually made of spun thread, made by insect grubs to protect themselves while they are transforming into adults

dhoti length of cloth, worn by Indian men, that can be wrapped around the body like a skirt or like baggy pants

doublets tight fitting jackets worn in Europe during the sixteenth century

felt thick cloth made of boiled, compressed wool or animal hair

flappers rebellious young women in 1920s Europe and the United States, so named because their short dresses flapped when they danced the Charleston and other popular dances of their day

girdle decorative band (usually braid or ribbon) worn to fasten a garment around the waist

hides the skins of cattle and other large animals, such as deer or buffalo

himation ancient Greek long cloak

gauze fine, transparent fabric, often woven from silk threads

jubba Syrian name for a long loose robe, worn as an outer garment in many North African and West Asian countries

kaftan long coat, opening at the front, originating in Persia (now Iran) and worn by many Asian peoples

loincloths strips of fabric wound around the hips and between the legs like a diaper.

mammilare band of fabric worn by women in ancient Rome to cover and support, much like a bra today

palla cloak worn by women in ancient Rome

parka hooded jacket, originally a fur-lined tunic worn by the Aleut people of the western Arctic region. Now worn with a button or zippered front by many in northern climates, especially in the northern United States. *See* anorak.

peers social equals or people of the same age and social group

peplos long robe worn by women in ancient Greece, made of a length of cloth that is wound around the body and folded over at the top to create a double layer of fabric covering the upper torso

ponchos South American cloaks, like blankets with a hole for the head.

sans-culottes nickname for political revolutionaries in eighteenth-century France who wore baggy pants or kilts of rough linen, as opposed to wealthy nobles who wore tailored culottes called knee breeches

sarongs lengths of wide cloth wrapped around bodies, worn by men and women in many parts of Southeast Asia

sinews tendons, which are stretchy bands that attach muscles to bones

stola outer tunic worn by women in ancient Rome

surcoat over-dress (for women); over-tunic (for men)

tailored cut and sewn to fit the shape of the body

toga a loosely wrapped cloak shaped like a half circle, worn in ancient Rome.

trunk hose short, thigh-length pants, fastened at the bottom to create a pouched or puffed effect, worn in sixteenth century Europe

tunics simple slip-on tops, usually going down to the knees or longer, that were either with or without sleeves, belted at the waist, and worn at various times as an undergarment or an outer garment

utility a style of clothing worn in Europe during and immediately after World War II

wimples bands of cloth covering women's necks from ear to ear and from the collarbone to the chin, worn in medieval Europe

Answers

Page 5: they were recycled as rags or bandages.
Page 6: animal **sinews** or lengths of hair from animals' manes and tails
Page 9: crisp, cool, white linen, which the Egyptians believed the gods wore in heaven
Page 11: by weaving each length of cloth specially for the person who would wear it
Page 13: adjustable fastenings — otherwise fitted styles would have been impossible to put on or take off
Page 15: they wore jackets padded with cotton wadding
Page 17: tie-dye indigo (blue) cloth made by Yoruba women of southwestern Nigeria
Page 19: brightly colored glass beads
Page 21: France
Page 23: chain-stitch machines were invented in 1858; lock-stitch machines in 1860
Page 25: "waist overalls"
Page 27: pantyhose. Before the 1960s, most Western women wore stockings and garter belts.
Page 29: Lycra, to improve the fit

Index